KNOTS, SPLICES, AND ROPE WORK

KNOTS, SPLICES, AND ROPE WORK

An Illustrated Handbook

A. Hyatt Verrill

Second Revised Edition

STERLING INNOVATION
New York

STERLING INNOVATION
New York

An Imprint of Sterling Publishing
387 Park Avenue South
New York, NY 10016

STERLING INNOVATION and the distinctive Sterling Innovation logo are registered trademarks of
Sterling Publishing Co., Inc.

This 2012 edition published by Sterling Innovation
Originally published in 1917 by the Norman W. Henley Publishing Company

All rights reserved. No part of this publication may be reproduced, stored in a retrieval system,
or transmitted, in any form or by any means, electronic, mechanical, photocopying, recording, or
otherwise, without prior written permission from the publisher.

Cover and box design: Jo Obarowski

ISBN 978-1-4027-9611-1

This book is part of *The Knots Box* kit and is not to be sold separately.

For information about custom editions, special sales, and premium and corporate purchases,
please contact Sterling Special Sales at 800-805-5489 or specialsales@sterlingpublishing.com.

Distributed in Canada by Sterling Publishing
c/o Canadian Manda Group, 165 Dufferin Street
Toronto, Ontario, Canada M6K 3H6
Distributed in the United Kingdom by GMC Distribution Services
Castle Place, 166 High Street, Lewes, East Sussex, England BN7 1XU
Distributed in Australia by Capricorn Link (Australia) Pty. Ltd.
P.O. Box 704, Windsor, NSW 2756, Australia

For information about custom editions, special sales, and premium and corporate purchases,
please contact Sterling Special Sales at 800-805-5489 or specialsales@sterlingpublishing.com.

Manufactured in China

Lot#
2 4 6 8 10 9 7 5 3 1
07/12

CONTENTS

Contents

INTRODUCTION

The history of ropes and knots is so dim and ancient that really little is known of their origin. That earliest man used cordage of some kind and by his ingenuity succeeded in tying the material together, is indisputable, for the most ancient carvings and decorations of prehistoric man show knots in several forms. Doubtless the trailing vines and plants first suggested ropes to human beings; and it is quite probable that these same vines, in their various twistings and twinings, gave man his first idea of knots.

Since the earliest times knots have been everywhere interwoven with human affairs; jugglers have used them in their tricks; they have become a part of many occupations and trades, while in song and story they have become the symbol of steadfastness and strength.

Few realize the importance that knots and cordage have played in the world's history, but if it had not been for these simple and every-day things, which as a rule are given far too little consideration, the human race could never have developed beyond savages. Indeed, I am not sure but it would be safe to state that the real difference between civilized and savage man consists largely in the knowledge of knots and rope work. No cloth could be woven, no net or seine knitted, no bow strung and no craft sailed on lake or sea without numerous knots and proper lines or ropes; and Columbus himself would have been far more handicapped without knots than without a compass.

History abounds with mention of knots, and in the eighth book of "Odyssey" Ulysses is represented as securing various articles of raiment by a rope fastened in a "knot closed with Circean art"; and as further proof of the prominence the ancients gave to knots the famous Gordian Knot may be mentioned. Probably no one will ever learn just how this fabulous knot was tied, and like many modern knots it was doubtless far easier for Alexander to cut it than to untie it.

The old sorcerers used knots in various ways, and the witches of Lapland sold sailors so-called "Wind Knots," which were untied by the sailors when they desired a particular wind. Even modern conjurors and wizards use knots extensively in their exhibitions and upon the accuracy and manner in which their knots are tied depends the success of their tricks.

In heraldry many knots have been used as symbols and badges and many old Coats of Arms bear intricate and handsome knots, or entwined ropes, emblazoned upon them.

As to the utility of knots and rope work there can be no question. A little knowledge of knots has saved many a life in storm and wreck, and if every one knew how to quickly and securely tie a knot there would be far fewer casualties in hotel and similar fires. In a thousand ways and times a knowledge of rope and knots is useful and many times necessary. Many an accident has occurred through a knot or splice being improperly formed, and even in tying an ordinary bundle or "roping" a trunk or box few people tie a knot that is secure and yet readily undone and quickly made. In a life of travel and adventure in out-of-the-way places, in yachting or boating, in hunting or fishing, and even in motoring, to command a number of good knots and splices is to make life safer, easier, and more enjoyable, aside from the real pleasure one may find in learning the interesting art of knot-tying.

Through countless ages the various forms of knots and fastenings for rope, cable, or cord have been developed; the best kinds being steadily improved and handed down from generation to generation, while the poor or inferior fastenings have been discarded by those whose callings required the use of cordage.

Gradually, too, each profession or trade has adopted the knots best suited to its requirements, and thus we find the Sailor's Knot; the Weaver's Knot; Fishermen's knots; Builders' knots; Butchers' knots; and many others which have taken their names from the use to which they are especially adapted.

In addition to these useful knots, there are many kinds of ornamental or fancy knots used in ornamenting the ends of ropes, decorating shrouds of vessels, railings, and similar objects; while certain braids or plaits, formed by a series of knots, are widely used aboard ship and on land.

In many cases ropes or cable must be joined in such a way that they present a smooth and even surface and for such purposes splices are used, while knots used merely as temporary fastenings and which must be readily and quickly tied and untied are commonly known as "bends" or "hitches." Oddly enough, it is far easier to tie a poor knot than a good one, and in ninety-nine cases out of a hundred the tyro, when attempting to join two ropes together, will tie either a "slippery" or a "jamming" knot and will seldom succeed in making a recognized and "ship-shape" knot of any sort.

The number of knots, ties, bends, hitches, splices, and shortenings in use is almost unlimited and they are most confusing and bewildering to the uninitiated. The most useful and ornamental, as well as the most reliable, are comparatively few in number, and in reality each knot learned leads readily to another; in the following pages I have endeavored to describe them in such a manner that their construction may be readily understood and mastered.

THE AUTHOR.
APRIL, 1912.

CHAPTER I

CORDAGE

Before taking up the matter of knots and splices in detail it may be well to give attention to cordage in general. Cordage, in its broadest sense, includes all forms and kinds of rope, string, twine, cable, etc., formed of braided or twisted strands. In making a rope or line the fibres (*A*, Fig. 1) of hemp, jute, cotton, or other material are loosely twisted together to form what is technically known as a "yarn" (*B*, Fig. 1). When two or more yarns are twisted together they form a "strand" (*C*, Fig. 1). Three or more strands form a rope (*D*, Fig. 1), and three ropes form a cable (*E*, Fig. 1). To form a strand the yarns are twisted together in the opposite direction from that in which the original fibres were twisted; to form a rope the strands are twisted in the opposite direction from the yarns of the strands, and, to form a cable each rope is twisted opposite from the twist of the strands. In this way the natural tendency for each yarn, strand, or rope to untwist serves to bind or hold the whole firmly together (Fig.1).

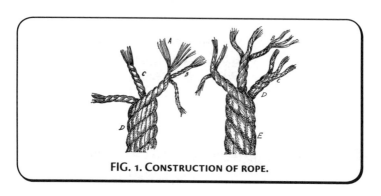

FIG. 1. CONSTRUCTION OF ROPE.

Rope is usually three-stranded and the strands turn from left to right or "with the sun," while cable is left-handed or twisted "against the sun" (*E*, Fig. 1). Certain ropes, such as "bolt-rope" and most cables, are laid around a "core" (*F*, Fig. 2) or central strand and in many cases are four-stranded (Fig. 2).

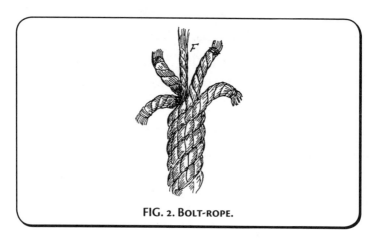

FIG. 2. BOLT-ROPE.

The strength of a rope depends largely upon the strength and length of the fibres from which it is made, but the amount each yarn and strand is twisted, as well as the method used in bleaching or preparing the fibres, has much to do with the strength of the finished line.

Roughly, the strength of ropes may be calculated by multiplying the circumference of the rope in inches by itself and the fifth part of the product will be the number of tons the rope will sustain. For example, if the rope is 5 inches in circumference, 5 X 5 = 25, one-fifth of which is 5, the number of tons that can safely be carried on a 5-inch rope. To ascertain the weight of ordinary "right hand" rope, multiply the circumference in inches by itself and multiply, the result by the length of rope in fathoms and divide the product by 3.75. For example, to find the weight of a 5-inch rope, 50 fathoms in length: 5 X 5 = 25; 25 x 50 = 1,250; 1,250 / 3.75 = 333-1/3 lbs. These figures apply to Manila or hemp rope, which is the kind commonly used, but jute, sisal-flax, grass, and silk are also used considerably. Cotton rope is seldom used save for small hand-lines, clothes-lines, twine, etc., while wire rope is largely used nowadays for rigging vessels, derricks, winches, etc., but as splicing wire rope is different from the method employed in fibre rope, and as knots have no place in wire rigging, we will not consider it.

Chapter II

SIMPLE KNOTS
AND BENDS

For convenience in handling rope and learning the various knots, ties, and bends, we use the terms "standing part," "bight," and "end" (Fig. 3). The *Standing Part* is the principal portion or longest part of the rope; the *Bight* is the part curved or bent while working or handling; while the *End* is that part used in forming the knot or hitch. Before commencing work the loose ends or strands of a rope should be "whipped" or "seized" to prevent the rope from unravelling; and although an expert can readily tie almost any knot, make a splice, or in fact do pretty nearly anything with a loose-ended rope, yet it is a wise plan to invariably whip the end of every rope, cable, or hawser to be handled, while a marline-spike, fid, or pointed stick will also prove of great help in working rope.

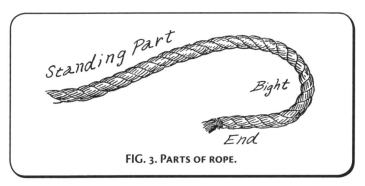

FIG. 3. PARTS OF ROPE.

To whip or seize a rope-end, take a piece of twine or string and lay it on the rope an inch or two from the end, pass the twine several times around the rope, keeping the ends of the twine under the first few turns to hold it in place; then make a large loop with the free end of twine; bring it back to the rope and continue winding for three or four turns around both rope and end of twine; and then finish by drawing the loop tight by pulling on the free end (Fig. 4).

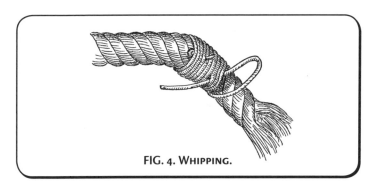

FIG. 4. WHIPPING.

All knots are begun by "loops" or rings commonly known to mariners as "Cuckolds' Necks" (Fig. 5). These may be either overhand or underhand, and when a seizing or fastening of twine is placed around the two parts where they cross a useful rope ring known as a "clinch" is formed (Fig. 6). If the loose end of the rope is passed over the standing part and through the "cuckold's-neck," the simplest of all knots, known as the "Overhand Knot," is made (Fig. 7). This drawn tight appears as in Fig. 8, and while so simple this knot is important, as it is frequently used in fastening the ends of yarns and strands in splicing, whipping, and seizing. The "Figure-Eight Knot" is almost as simple as the overhand and is plainly shown in Figs. 9 and 10. Only a step beyond the figure-eight and the overhand knots are the "Square" and "Reefing" knots (Figs. 11 and 12). The square knot is probably the most useful and widely used of any common knot and is the best all-around knot known. It is very strong, never slips or becomes jammed, and is readily untied. To make a square knot, take the ends of

the rope and pass the left end over and under the right end, then the right over and under the left. If you once learn the simple formula of "Left over," "Right over," you will never make a mistake and form the despised "Granny," a most useless, bothersome, and deceptive makeshift for any purpose

(Fig. 13). The true "Reef Knot" is merely the square knot with the bight of the left or right end used instead of the end itself. This enables the knot to be "cast off" more readily than the regular square knot (*A*, Fig. 12). Neither square nor reef knots, however, are reliable when tying two ropes of unequal size together, for under such conditions they will frequently slip and appear as in Fig. 14, and sooner or later will pull apart. To prevent this the ends may be tied or seized as shown in Fig. 15. A better way to join two ropes of unequal diameter is to use the "Open-and Knot." This knot is shown in Fig. 16, and is very quickly and easily made; it never slips or gives, but is rather large and clumsy, and if too great a strain is put on the rope it is more likely to break at the knot than at any other spot. The "Fisherman's Knot," shown in Fig. 17, is a good knot and is formed by two simple overhand knots slipped over each rope, and when drawn taut appears as in Fig. 18. This is an important and valuable knot for anglers, as the two lines may be drawn apart by taking hold of the ends, *A*, *B*, and a third line for a sinker, or extra hook, may be inserted between them. In joining gut lines the knot should be left slightly open and the space between wrapped with silk. This is probably the strongest known method of fastening fine lines.

FIG. 5. CUCKOLDS' NECKS.

FIG. 6. CLINCH.

FIGS. 7 AND 8. OVERHAND KNOTS.

FIGS. 9 AND 10. FIGURE-EIGHT KNOTS.

FIGS. 11 AND 12. SQUARE KNOTS.

FIG. 13. GRANNY KNOT.

FIG. 14. SLIPPED SQUARE KNOT.

FIG. 15. SQUARE KNOT WITH ENDS SEIZED.

FIG. 16. OPEN-HAND KNOTS.

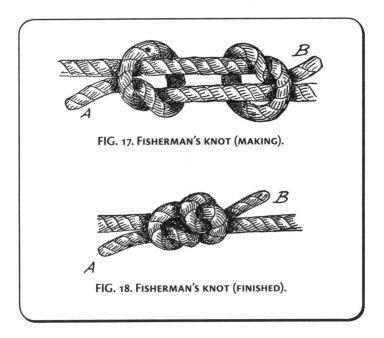

FIG. 17. FISHERMAN'S KNOT (MAKING).

FIG. 18. FISHERMAN'S KNOT (FINISHED).

The "Ordinary Knot," for fastening heavy ropes, is shown in Fig. 19. It is made by forming a simple knot and then interlacing the other rope or "following around," as shown in Fig. 20. This knot is very strong, will not slip, is easy to make, and does not strain the fibres of the rope. Moreover, ropes joined with this knot will pay out, or hang, in a straight line. By whipping the ends to the standing parts it becomes a neat and handsome knot (Fig. 21). The "Weaver's Knot" (Fig. 22) is more useful in joining small lines, or twine, than for rope, and for thread it is without doubt the best knot known. The ends are crossed as in Fig. 23. The end *A* is then looped back over the end *B*, and the end *B* is slipped through loop *C* and drawn tight.

FIG. 19. Ordinary knot (finished).

FIG. 20. Ordinary knot (tying).

FIG. 21. Ordinary knot (seized).

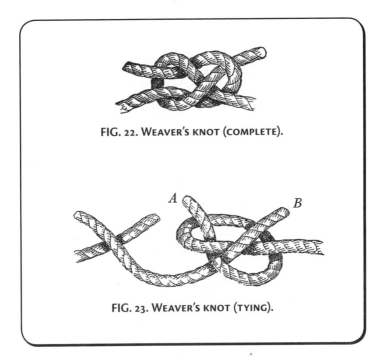

FIG. 22. Weaver's knot (complete).

FIG. 23. Weaver's knot (tying).

Another useful and handsome knot is illustrated in Fig. 24. This is a variation of the figure-eight knot, already described, and is used where there is too much rope, or where a simple knot is desired to prevent the rope running through an eye, ring, or tackle-block. It is made by forming a regular figure eight and then "following round" with the other rope as in Fig. 25. It is then drawn taut and the ends seized to the standing part if desired.

FIG. 24. DOUBLE FIGURE-EIGHT KNOT (COMPLETE).

FIG. 25. DOUBLE FIGURE-EIGHT KNOT (TYING).

Sometimes we have occasion to join two heavy or stiff ropes or hawsers, and for this purpose the "Garrick Bend" (Fig. 26) is preeminently the best of all knots. To make this knot, form a bight by laying the end of a rope on top of and across the standing part. Next take the end of the other rope and pass it through this bight, first down, then up, over the cross and down through the bight again, so that it comes out on the opposite side from the other end, thus bringing one end on top and the other below, as illustrated in Fig. 27. If the lines are very stiff or heavy the knot may be secured by seizing the ends to the standing parts. A much simpler and a far poorer knot is sometimes used in fastening two heavy ropes together. This is a simple hitch within a loop, as illustrated in Fig. 28, but while it has the advantage of being quickly and easily tied it is so inferior to the Garrick bend that I advise all to adopt the latter in its place.

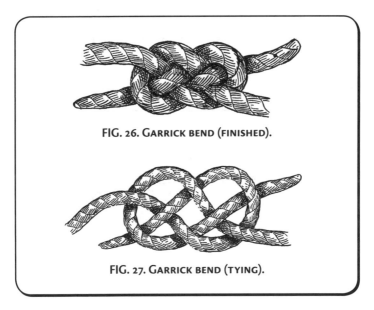

FIG. 26. Garrick bend (finished).

FIG. 27. Garrick bend (tying).

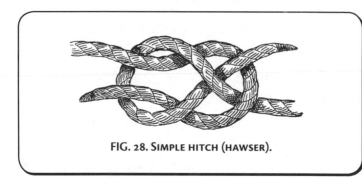

FIG. 28. SIMPLE HITCH (HAWSER).

When two heavy lines are to be fastened for any considerable time, a good method is to use the "Half-hitch and Seizing," shown in Fig. 29. This is a secure and easy method of fastening ropes together and it allows the rope to be handled more easily, and to pass around a winch or to be coiled much more readily, than when other knots are used.

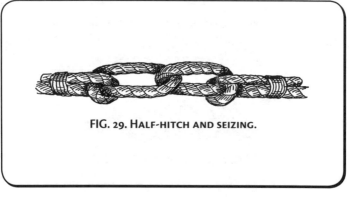

FIG. 29. HALF-HITCH AND SEIZING.

CHAPTER III

TIES AND HITCHES

All the knots I have so far described are used mainly for fastening the two ends of a rope, or of two ropes, together. Of quite a different class are the knots used in making a rope fast to a stationary or solid object, and are known as "hitches" or "ties."

One of the easiest of this class to make and one which is very useful in fastening a boat or other object where it may be necessary to release it quickly is the "Lark's Head" (Fig. 30). To make this tie, pass a bight of our rope through the ring, or other object, to which you are making fast and then pass a marline-spike, a billet of wood, or any similar object through the sides of the bight and under or behind the standing part, as shown in *A*, Fig. 30. The end of the rope may then be laid over and under the standing part and back over itself. This knot may be instantly released by merely pulling out the toggle. Almost as quickly made and unfastened is the "Slippery Hitch" (Fig. 32). To make this, run the end of the rope through the ring or eye to which it is being fastened, then back over the standing part and pull a loop, or bight, back through the "cuckold's neck" thus formed (Fig. 33). To untie, merely pull on the free end. Two half-hitches, either around a post or timber or around the standing part of the rope, make an ideal and quickly tied fastening (Figs. 34 and 35). To make these, pass the end around the post, ring, or other object, then over and around the standing part between the post and itself, then under and around the standing part and between its own loop and the first one formed. After a little practice you can tie this knot almost instantly and by merely throwing a couple of turns around a post, two half-hitches may be formed instantly. This knot will hold forever without loosening, and even on a smooth, round stick or spar it will stand an enormous strain without slipping. A more secure knot for this same purpose is the "Clove Hitch" (Fig. 36), sometimes known as the "Builders' Hitch." To make this, pass the end of rope around the spar or timber, then over itself; over and around the spar, and pass the end under itself and between rope and spar, as shown in the illustration. The Clove hitch with ends knotted becomes the "Gunners' Knot" (Fig. 37). These are among the most valuable and important of knots and are useful in a thousand and one places. The Clove hitch will hold fast on a smooth timber and is used extensively by builders for fastening the stageing to the upright posts. It is also useful in making a tow-line fast to a wet spar, or timber, and even on a slimy and slippery spile it will seldom slip. For this purpose the "Timber Hitch" (Fig. 38) is even better than the Clove hitch. It is easily made by passing the end of a rope around the spar or log, round the standing part of the rope and then twist it three or more times around, under and over itself. If you wish this still more secure, a single half-hitch may be taken with the line a couple of feet further along the spar (Fig. 39).

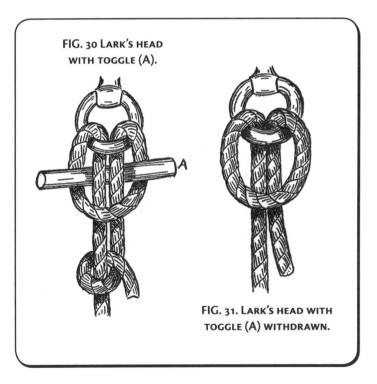

FIG. 30 LARK'S HEAD WITH TOGGLE (A).

FIG. 31. LARK'S HEAD WITH TOGGLE (A) WITHDRAWN.

FIG. 32. SLIPPERY HITCH (COMPLETE).

B

FIG. 33. SLIPPERY HITCH (TYING).

FIG. 34. HALF-HITCHES.

FIG. 35. CLOVE HITCH OR
BUILDER'S HITCH (TYING).

FIG. 36 A. CLOVE HITCH OR BUILDERS HITCH (TYING)

FIG. 36 B. CLOVE HITCH (COMPLETE)

FIG. 37. GUNNER'S KNOT.

FIG. 38. TIMBER HITCH.

FIG. 39. TIMBER HITCH AND HALF-HITCH.

It is remarkable what power to grip a twisted rope has, and the "Twist Knots" shown in Figs. 40 and 41 illustrate two ways of making fast which are really not knots at all but merely twists. These may be finished by a simple knot, or a bow-knot, as shown in Fig. 42, but they are likely to jam under great pressure and are mainly useful in tying packages, or bundles, with small cord, where the line must be held taut until the knot is completed. This principle of fastening by twisted rope is also utilized in the "Cat-spaw" (Fig. 43), a most useful knot or "hitch" for hoisting with a hook. To make this, pass the bight of your rope over the end and standing part, then, with a bight in each hand, take three twists from you, then bring the two bights side by side and throw over the hook (Fig. 44).

FIGS. 40 AND 41. "TWISTS."

FIG. 42. TWIST WITH BOW.

FIG. 43. CATSPAW.

FIG. 44. CATSPAW (TYING).

The "Blackwall Hitch" (Fig. 45) is still simpler and easier to make and merely consists of a loop, or cuckold's neck, with the end of rope passed underneath the standing part and across the hook so that as soon as pressure is exerted the standing part bears on the end and jams it against the hook.

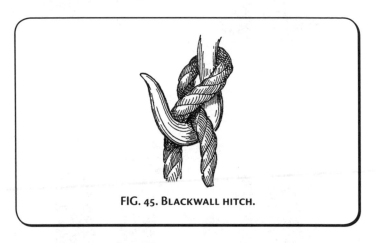

FIG. 45. BLACKWALL HITCH.

The "Chain Hitch" (Fig. 46) is a very strong method of fastening a line to a timber, or large rope, where one has a rope of sufficient length, and is used frequently to help haul in a large rope or for similar purposes. It consists simply of a number of half-hitches taken at intervals around the object and is sometimes used with a lever or handspike, as shown in Fig. 47. The "Rolling Hitch" is a modified Clove hitch and is shown in

Fig. 48. The "Magnus Hitch" (Fig. 49) is a method frequently used on shipboard for holding spars; and the "Studding-sail Bend" (Fig. 50) is also used for this purpose. Occasions sometimes arise where a tackle, hook, ring, or another rope must be fastened to a beam by the same rope being used, and in such cases the "Roband Hitch" (Fig. 51) comes in very handy. These are all so simple and easily understood from the figures that no explanation is necessary. Almost as simple are the "Midshipman's Hitch" (Fig. 52), the "Fisherman's Hitch" (Fig. 53), and the "Gaff Topsail Halyard Bend" (Fig. 54). The midshipman's hitch is made by taking a half-hitch around the standing part and a round turn twice around above it. The fisherman's hitch is particularly useful in making fast large hawsers; with the end of a rope take two turns around a spar, or through a ring; take a half-hitch around the standing part and under all the turns; then a half-hitch round the standing part only and if desired seize the end to standing part. The gaff-topsail bend is formed by passing two turns around the yard and coming up on a third turn over both the first two turns; over its own part and one turn; then stick the end under the first turn.

FIG 46. CHAIN HITCH.

FIG. 47. CHAIN HITCH WITH BAR.

FIG. 48. ROLLING HITCH.

FIG. 49. MAGNUS HITCH.

FIG. 50. STUDDING-SAIL BEND.

**FIG. 51 A. ROBAND HITCH
(FRONT).**

**FIG. 51 B. ROBAND HITCH
(BACK).**

FIG. 52. MIDSHIPMAN'S HITCH.

FIG. 53. FISHERMAN'S HITCH.

FIG. 54. GAFF-TOPSAIL HALYARD BEND.

CHAPTER IV

NOOSES, LOOPS, AND MOORING KNOTS

Nothing is more interesting to a landsman than the manner in which a sailor handles huge, dripping hawsers or cables and with a few deft turns makes then fast to a pier-head or spile, in such a way that the ship's winches, warping the huge structure to or from the dock, do not cause the slightest give or slip to the rope and yet, a moment later, with a few quick motions, the line is cast off, tightened up anew, or paid out as required. Clove hitches, used as illustrated in Fig. 55, and known as the "Waterman's Knot," are often used, with a man holding the free end, for in this way a slight pull holds the knot fast, while a little slack gives the knot a chance to slip without giving way entirely and without exerting any appreciable pull on the man holding the end.

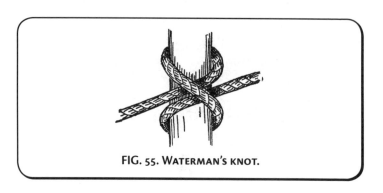

FIG. 55. WATERMAN'S KNOT.

"Larks' Heads" are also used in conjunction with a running noose, as shown in Fig. 56, while a few turns under and over and around a cleat, or about two spiles, is a method easily understood and universally used by sailors (Fig. 57). The sailor's knot par excellence, however, is the "Bow-line" (Fig. 58), and wherever we find sailors, or seamen, we will find this knot in one or another of its various forms. When you can readily and surely tie this knot every time, you may feel yourself on the road to "Marline-spike Seamanship," for it is a true sailor's knot and never slips, jams, or fails; is easily and quickly untied, and is useful in a hundred places around boats or in fact in any walk of life. The knot in its various stages is well shown in Fig. 59 and by following these illustrations you will understand it much better than by a description alone. In *A* the rope is shown with a bight or cuckold's neck formed with the end over the standing part. Pass *A* back through the bight, under, then over, then under, as shown in *B*, then over and down through the bight, as shown in *C* and *D*, and draw taut, as in *E*. The "Bow-line on a Bight" (Fig. 60) is just as easily made and is very useful in slinging casks or barrels and in forming a seat for men to be lowered over cliffs, or buildings, or to be hoisted aloft aboard ship for painting, cleaning, or rigging. A "Running Bow-line" (Fig. 61) is merely a bow-line with the end passed through the loop, thus forming a slip knot. Other "Loops" are made as shown in Figs. 62–65, but none of these are as safe, sure, and useful as the bow-line. One of these knots, known as the "Tomfool Knot" (Fig. 66), is used as handcuffs and has become quite famous, owing to its having baffled a number of "Handcuff Kings" and other performers who readily escaped from common knots and manacles. It is made like the running knot (Fig. 62), and the firm end is then passed through the open, simple knot so as to form a double loop or bow. If the hands or wrists are placed within these loops and the latter drawn taut, and the loose ends tied firmly around the central part, a pair of wonderfully secure handcuffs results.

FIG. 56. LARKS' HEADS AND RUNNING NOOSE.

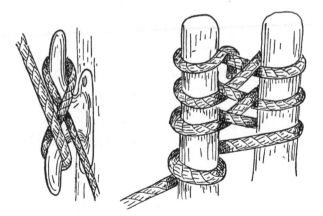

FIG. 57. CLEAT AND WHARF TIES.

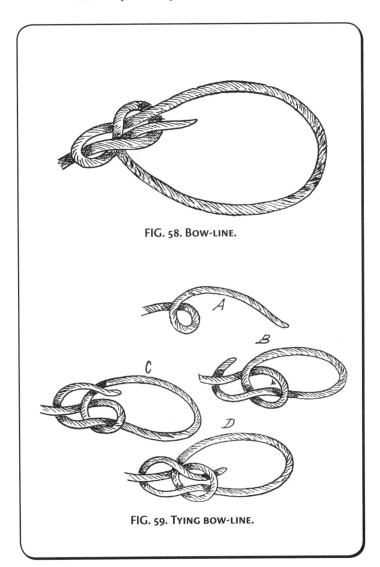

FIG. 58. Bow-line.

FIG. 59. Tying bow-line.

FIG. 60. BOW-LINE ON BIGHT.

FIG. 61. RUNNING BOW-LINE.

FIG. 62. LOOP KNOT.

FIG. 63. LOOP KNOT.

FIG. 64. LOOP KNOT.

FIG. 65. LOOP KNOT.

FIG. 66. TOMFOOL KNOT.

CHAPTER V
SHORTENINGS, GROMMETS, AND SELVAGEES

In many cases a rope may prove too long for our use or the free ends may be awkward, or in the way. At such times a knowledge of "shortenings" is valuable. There are quite a variety of these useful knots, nearly all of which are rather handsome and ornamental, in fact a number of them are in constant use aboard ship merely for ornament.

The simplest form of shortening, shown in Fig. 67, is a variation of the common and simple overhand knot already described and illustrated. These knots are formed by passing the end of a rope twice or more times through the loop of the simple knot and then drawing it tight (Fig. 68). They are known as "Double," "Treble," "Fourfold," or "Sixfold" knots and are used to prevent a rope from passing through a ring or block as well as for shortening. All gradations from the double to the sixfold are shown in Fig. 69, both in process of making and as they appear when drawn taut. Another very simple form of shortening is shown in Fig. 70 and is known as the "Single Plait," or "Chain Knot." To make this shortening, make a running loop (*A*, Fig. 70), then draw a bight of the rope through this loop, as shown at *B*, draw another bight through this, as at *C* to *D*, and continue in this way until the rope is shortened to the desired length; the free end should then be fastened by passing a bit of stick through the last loop, *F*, or by running the free end through the last loop, as at *E*. To undo this shortening, it is only necessary to slip out the free end, or the bit of wood, and pull on the end, when the entire knot will quickly unravel. The "Twist," or "Double Chain," is made in a similar manner but is commenced in a different way (*A*, Fig. 71). It may also be made with three separate pieces of line, as shown in *B*, Fig. 71. Hold the double loop in the left hand; the part *A* is then brought over *B*; with a half turn *B* is crossed over to *A*, and then proceed as in the ordinary three-strand plait until the end of loop is reached, when the loose end is fastened by passing through the bight and the completed shortening appears as in Fig. 72. This same process is often used by Mexicans and Westerners in making bridles, headstalls, etc., of leather. The leather to be used is slit lengthwise from near one end to near the other, as shown in Fig. 73, and the braid is formed as described. The result appears as in Fig. 74, and in this way the ends of the leather strap remain uncut, and thus much stronger and neater than they would be were three separate strips used.

FIG. 67. TWOFOLD SHORTENING (MAKING).   **FIG. 68 TWOFOLD SHORTENING (TAUT)**

FIG. 69. THREE- AND FIVEFOLD SHORTENING.

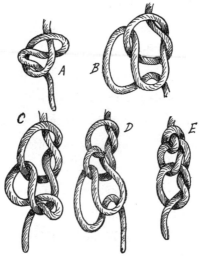

FIG. 70. SINGLE PLAIT OR MONKEY CHAIN (MAKING).

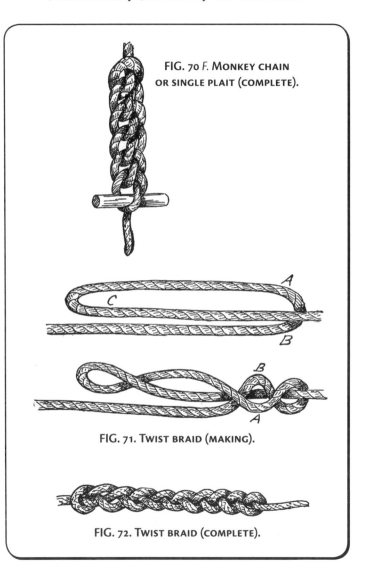

FIG. 70 F. MONKEY CHAIN OR SINGLE PLAIT (COMPLETE).

FIG. 71. TWIST BRAID (MAKING).

FIG. 72. TWIST BRAID (COMPLETE).

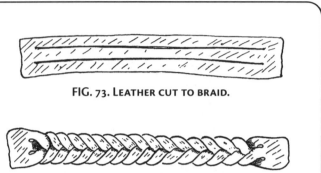

FIG. 73. LEATHER CUT TO BRAID.

FIG. 74. LEATHER BRAID (COMPLETE).

Another handsome knot for shortening is the more highly ornamental "Open Chain" (Fig. 75). Make the first loop of the rope secure by a twist of the rope and then pass the loose end through the preceding loop, to right and left alternately, until the knot is complete.

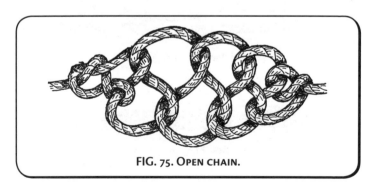

FIG. 75. OPEN CHAIN.

Shortenings, Grommets, and Selvagees

The simplest of all shortenings consists of a loop taken in the rope with the bights seized to the standing part (Fig. 76). This is particularly well adapted to heavy rope or where a shortening must be made quickly. Fig. 77 shows another very simple shortening, which requires no description. This will not withstand a very great strain but is secure from untying by accident and is very useful for taking up spare rope of lashings on bundles or baggage. "Sheepshanks," or "Dogshanks," are widely used for shortening rope, especially where both ends are fast, as they can be readily made in the centre of a tied rope. There are several forms of these useful knots. The best and most secure form is shown in Fig. 78. A simple running knot is first made; a bend is pushed through the loop, which is then drawn taut; the other end of the bend is fastened in a similar manner and the shortening is complete. A much simpler form is shown in Fig. 79, but this can hardly be depended upon unless the ends are seized, as shown in Fig. 80. Figs. 81–82 illustrate two other forms of shortenings, but these can only be used where the end of the rope is free, and are intended for more permanent fastenings than the ordinary sheepshank; while Fig. 83 is particularly adapted to be cast loose at a moment's notice by jerking out the toggles, *A*, *B*.

FIG. 76. SEIZED SHORTENING.

FIG. 77. BOW SHORTENING.

FIG. 78. SHEEPSHANK.

FIG. 79. ANOTHER SHEEPSHANK.

FIG. 80. SHEEPSHANK WITH ENDS SEIZED.

FIG. 81. SHEEPSHANK FOR FREE-ENDED ROPE.

FIG. 82. SHEEPSHANK FOR FREE-ENDED ROPE.

FIG. 83. SHEEPSHANK WITH TOGGLE.

Grommets are round, endless rings of rope useful in a myriad ways aboard ship as well as ashore. They are often used as handles for chests, for rings with which to play quoits, to lengthen rope, and in many similar ways. The grommet is formed of a single strand of rope *five times as long as the circumference of the grommet when complete*. Take the strand and lay one end across the other at the size of loop required and with the long end follow the grooves or "lay" of the strand until back to where you started (Fig. 84), thus forming a two-stranded ring. Then continue twisting the free end between the turns already made until the three-strand ring is complete (Fig. 85). Now finish and secure the ends by making overhand knots, pass the ends underneath the nearest strands and trim ends off close (Fig. 86). If care is taken and you remember to keep a strong twist on the strand while "laying up" the grommet, the finished ring will be as firm and smooth and endless as the original rope.

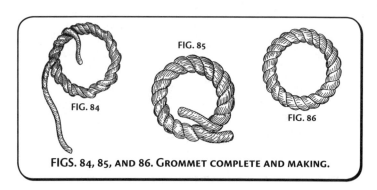

FIGS. 84, 85, AND 86. GROMMET COMPLETE AND MAKING.

A "Sevagee" or "Selvagee" strap is another kind of ring (Fig. 87). This is made by passing a number of strands or yarns around pins or nails set in a board (Fig. 88), and binding the whole together with a seizing of yarn or marline (Fig. 89). These are strong, durable straps much used for blocks aboard ship, for handles to boxes and chests, and in many similar ways. A "Flemish Eye" (Fig. 90) is an eye made in a manner much like that employed in forming the selvagee strap. Take a spar or piece of wood the size of the intended eye *A*. Around this wood lay a number of pieces of yarn or marline, *B*, *B*, *B*, and fasten them by tying with twine as at *C*. Whip the piece of rope in which eye is to be formed and unravel and open out the strands as at *D*. Lap the yarns over the wood and the stops *B*, and fasten together by overhand knots *E*, worm the free ends under and over and then bring up the ends of the stops *B* and tie around the strands of eye as shown. The eye may be finished neatly by whipping all around with yarn or marline, and will then appear as in Fig. 90 *B*. An "Artificial Eye" (Fig. 91) is still another form of eye which will be found useful and in some ways easier and quicker to make than a spliced eye, besides being stronger.

FIG. 87. Selvagee strap.

FIG. 88. Selvagee board.

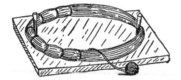

FIG. 89. Seizing a selvagee strap.

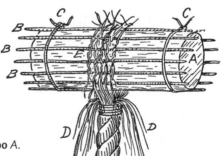

FIG. 90 *A*.
Making Flemish eye.

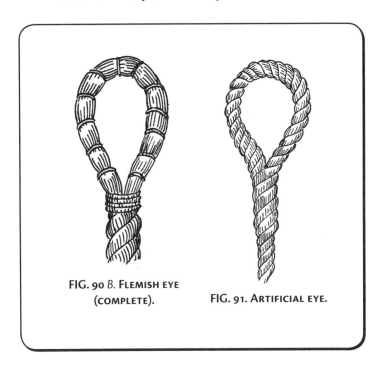

FIG. 90 *B*. Flemish eye
(complete).

FIG. 91. Artificial eye.

Take the end of a rope and unlay one strand; place the two remaining strands back alongside of the standing part (Fig. 92). Pass the loose strand which has been unlaid over the end, and follow around the spaces between the two strands and then around eye,—as in making a grommet,—until it returns down the standing part and lies under the eye with the strands (Fig. 93). Then divide the strands, taper them down, and whip the whole with yarn or marline (Fig. 94).

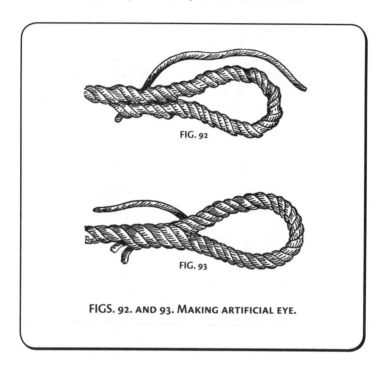

FIG. 92

FIG. 93

FIGS. 92. AND 93. MAKING ARTIFICIAL EYE.

Still another eye which at times will be useful is the "Throat Seizing," shown in Fig. 95. This is made by opening the end slightly and lashing it to the standing part as shown. Another ring sometimes used is illustrated in Fig. 96, and is easily and quickly made by lashing the two ends of a short rope to the standing part of another. Cuckolds' necks with lashings or "Clinches" are also used for the same purpose.

FIG. 94. ARTIFICIAL EYE (WHIPPED).

FIG. 95. THROAT SEIZING.

FIG. 96. LASHED CUT-SPLICE.

Chapter VI

LASHINGS, SEIZINGS, SPLICES, ETC.

Almost any one can lash a rope more or less satisfactorily, but a knowledge of how to do this properly and in the manner best suited to each case is of great importance to seamen and others having occasion to handle ropes, rigging, or in fact any cordage.

The varieties of lashings, seizings, whippings, and servings are almost innumerable, but a few of the best and most frequently used are the "Wedding Knot" or "Rose Lashing," the "Deadeye Lashing," the "Belaying-pin Splice," the "Necklace Tie," the "Close Band," and "End Pointings." The rose lashing (Fig. 97) is used to join two eyes or ropes finished with loops. The deadeye lashing (Fig. 98) is frequently, used on ships' standing rigging and is a familiar sight to every one who has seen a sailing-vessel. It consists of a small line reeved back and forth through the holes in the "deadeyes," *A*; the ends are then seized to the standing rigging to prevent slipping. This lashing admits of easy and rapid lengthening or shortening of the rigging and is particularly useful in connection with wire cable. A similar method may be used with loops instead of deadeyes (Fig. 99). The belaying-pin splice, shown in Fig. 100, is a quick and handy way of fastening two ropes together and is of great value when rigging is carried away and some quick method of joining the severed ends is required. Pass a belaying-pin or similar toggle through an eye or loop in one end of a rope and pass this through a loop or eye in the broken rope end. Form a loop in the other broken end, slip the free end of the lanyard through this and around another toggle or pin and haul taut; then fasten by half-hitches around standing part (*A*, Fig. 100), or by seizing (*B*, Fig. 100). This is a strong, reliable fastening and can be tightened up or instantly thrown off at will.

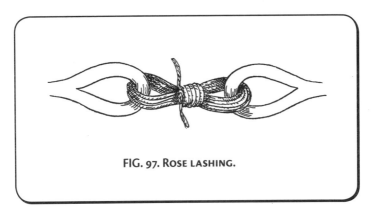

FIG. 97. ROSE LASHING.

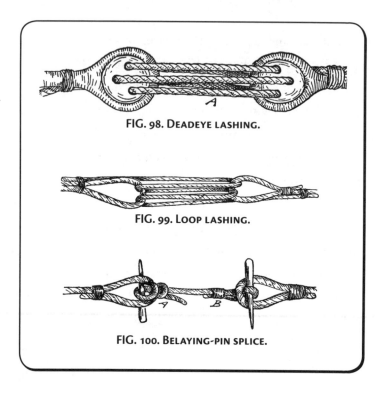

FIG. 98. DEADEYE LASHING.

FIG. 99. LOOP LASHING.

FIG. 100. BELAYING-PIN SPLICE.

The necklace tie is useful in holding two ropes, hawsers, or timbers side by side (Fig. 101). The lashing is passed around and around the two objects to be joined and the ends secured by a square knot passed around the band lengthwise. The close band is used for the same purposes as the last and is made in the same manner, but the ends are fastened by drawing through beneath the turns (Fig. 102).

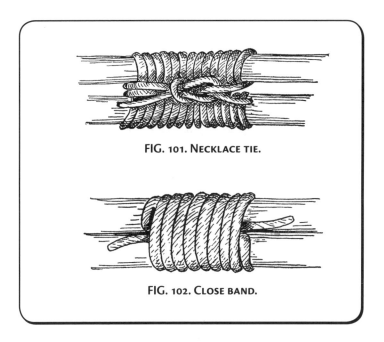

FIG. 101. NECKLACE TIE.

FIG. 102. CLOSE BAND.

End pointings are very useful as well as ornamental, for while an ordinary seizing or whipping will prevent the strands from unravelling, the ends are broad and clumsy and oftentimes are too large to pass through a block or eye large enough for the rest of the rope. The ordinary way of pointing a rope is to first whip as described (Fig. 4), and then unlay the end as for the Flemish eye. Take out about two-thirds of the yarns and twist each in two. Take two parts of different yarns and twist together with finger and thumb, keeping the lay on the yarn and thus forming left-handed stuff known as "nettles." Comb out the rest of the yarn with a knife, leaving a few to lay back upon the rope. Now pass three turns of twine like a timber-hitch tightly around the part where the nettles separate and fasten the twine, and while passing this "warp" lay the nettles backward and forward with each turn. The ends are now whipped with twine or yarn and finally "snaked," which is done by taking the end under and over the outer turns of the seizing alternately. If the rope is small a stick is often put in the upper part to strengthen it or the tip maybe finished with a small eye. If properly done a pointed rope is very handsome and appears as in *B*, Fig. 103. Another simple way of finishing a rope end is to seize the end, as at *A*, Fig. 104, and open out the strands, bring the strands back alongside the rope, and whip the whole (Fig. 105).

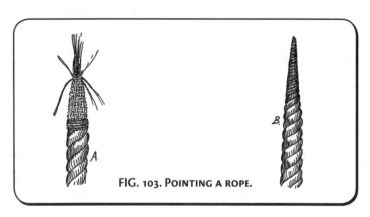

FIG. 103. Pointing a rope.

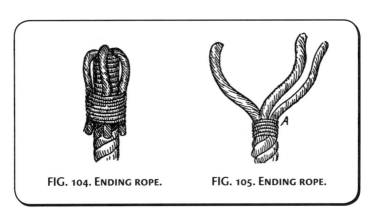

FIG. 104. ENDING ROPE.   **FIG. 105. ENDING ROPE.**

Splicing is, in many cases, more useful and better than tying or bending ropes together and a good splice always looks neater and more ship-shape than a knot, no matter how well-made it may be. A person familiar with splicing will turn in a splice almost as quickly as the ordinary man can tie a secure knot, and in many cases, where the rope must pass through sheaves or blocks, a splice is absolutely necessary to fasten two ropes or two parts of a parted rope together. The simplest of all splices is known as the "Short Splice" (Fig. 106). This is made as follows: Untwist the ends of the rope for a few inches and seize with twine to prevent further unwinding, as shown at *A, A*; also seize the end of each strand to prevent unravelling and grease or wax the strands until smooth and even. Now place the two ends of the ropes together as shown at *B, B*. Then with a marline-spike, or a pointed stick, work open the strand 1 *c*, and through this pass the strand *A* of the other rope; then open strand 2 and pass the next strand of the other rope through it and then the same way with the third strand. Next open up the strands of the other rope, below the seizing, and pass the strands of the first rope through as before, 3 *A*, *B*. The ropes will now appear as in Fig. 106, *D*. Now untwist the six strands and cut away about half the yarns from each and seize the ends as before; pass these reduced strands through under the whole strands of the rope— the strands of the left under the strands of the right rope and *vice versa*—for two or three lays and then cut off projecting ends, after drawing all as tight as you can. If an extra-neat splice is desired the strands should be gradually tapered as you proceed, and in this way a splice but little larger than the original diameter of the rope will result. The only difficulty you will find in making this splice is in getting the strands to come together in such a way that two strands will not run under the same strand of the opposite rope. To avoid this, bear in mind that the *first strand must be passed over the strand which is first next to it and through under the second and out between the second and third.* In the following operations the strands are passed *over* the third and *under* the fourth; but the figures will make this perfectly clear. A far better and stronger splice is the "Long Splice," which will run through any block or tackle which will dmit the rope itself; indeed, a well-made long splice cannot be distinguished from the rope itself after a few days' use (Fig. 107). To make this useful splice, unlay the ends of the rope about four times as much as for the short splice, or from four to five feet, unlay one strand in each rope for half as much again; place the middle strands together as at *A*, then the additional strands will appear as at *B* and *C*, and the spiral groove, left where they were unlaid, will appear as at *D* and *E*. Take off the two central strands, *F* and *G*, and lay them into the grooves, *D*, *E*, until they meet *B* and *C*, and be sure and keep them tightly twisted while so doing. Then take strands *H* and *J*, cut out half the yarns in each, make an overhand knot in them and tuck the ends under the next lays as in a short splice. Do the same with strands *B*, *C* and *F*, *G*; dividing, knotting, and sticking the divided strands in the same way. Finally stretch the rope tight, pull and pound and roll the splice until smooth and round, and trim off all loose ends close to the rope.

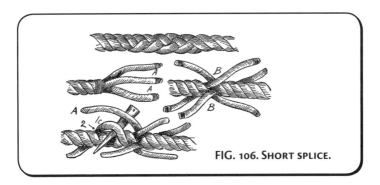

FIG. 106. SHORT SPLICE.

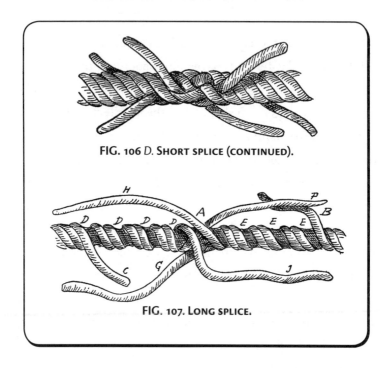

FIG. 106 *D.* **Short splice (continued).**

FIG. 107. Long splice.

An "Eye Splice" (Fig. 108) is very easy to make and is useful and handy in a great variety of ways. It is made in the same manner as the short splice, but instead of splicing the two ends together, the end of the rope is unlaid and then bent around and spliced into its own strands of the standing part, as shown in the illustration. A "Cut Splice" (Fig. 109) is made just as an eye splice or short splice, but instead of splicing two ropes together end to end, or splicing an end into a standing part, the ends are lapped and each is spliced into the standing part of the other, thus forming a loop or eye in the centre of a rope. Once the short and long splices are mastered, all other splices, as well as many useful variations, will come easy. Oftentimes, for example, one strand of a rope may become worn, frayed, or broken, while the remaining strands are perfectly sound. In such cases the weak strand may be unlaid and cut off and then a new strand of the same length is laid up in the groove left by the old strand exactly as in a long splice; the ends are then tapered, stuck under the lay, as in a short splice, and the repair is complete; and if well done will never show and will be as strong as the original rope.

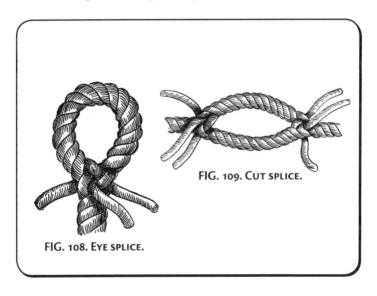

FIG. 109. CUT SPLICE.

FIG. 108. EYE SPLICE.

Chapter VII

FANCY KNOTS
AND ROPE WORK

The knots and splices described above are all more for practical use than ornament, although such shortenings as the Single and Double plaits, the Chain knots, the Twofold, Fourfold, and Sixfold knots, and others are often used for ornamental purposes only. A certain class of knots are, however, really ornamental and seldom serve to fasten two ropes together, or to make any object fast to another. They are, however, very useful in many ways, especially aboard ship, and they are so handsome and interesting that every one interested in rope work should learn to make them. The simplest of the fancy knots is known as the "Single Crown" (Fig. 110). To form this knot unlay the strands of a new, flexible rope for six to eight inches and whip the ends of each strand, as well as the standing part, to prevent further untwisting. Hold the rope in your left hand and fold one strand over and away from you, as shown in *A*, Fig. 111. Then fold the next strand over *A* (see *B*, Fig. 111), and then, while holding these in place with thumb and finger, pass the strand *C* over strand *B*, and through the bight of *A* as shown in the illustration. Now pull all ends tight and work the bights up smooth and snug; cut off ends and the knot s complete. This single crown is a very poor knot to stand by itself, however, and is mainly valuable as a basis for other more complicated knots and for ending up rope. To end up a rope with a crown it is merely necessary to leave the projecting ends long and then by bringing them down tuck under the strands of the standing part, as shown in Fig. 112. Then halve the strands and tuck again, as in making a short splice, until the result appears as in Fig. 113. This makes a neat, handy, and ship-shape finish to a rope's end and is very useful for painters, halyards, etc. It will never work loose like a seizing and is quickly put on at any time, whereas to make a seizing one must be provided with small stuff of some sort, and this is frequently not at hand. The "Wall Knot" (Fig. 114) is almost as simple as the crown, and in fact is practically a crown reversed. In making this knot bring *C* downward and across the standing part; then bring *A* over *C* and around standing part and finally bring *B* over *A* and up through bight of *C*, Fig. 115. When drawn snug the ends may be trimmed off close or they may be tucked and tapered as in the crown and will then appear as in Fig. 116. As in the case of the crown knot, the wall is mainly of value as an ending when ends are tucked, or as a basis for more ornamental knots such as the "Wall and Crown," or "Double Wall," or "Double Crown." It is also very largely used in making "Shroud Knots" (Fig. 117). The common shroud knot is made by opening up the strands of a rope's end as for a short splice and placing the two ends together in the same way. Then single "wall" the strands of one rope around the standing part of another against the lay, taper the ends, and tuck and serve all with yarn or marline (Fig. 118). The "French Shroud Knot" is far neater and better, but is a little harder to make. Open up the strands and place closely together as for the short splice; make a loop of strand *A*, pass the end of *B* through the bight of *A*, as at *C*, make a loop of strand *D*, and pass the end of strand *A* through it as at *D*; then pass the end of strand *D* through the bight of strand *B* and one side is complete. Repeat the operation on the other side, draw all ends taut, and taper and tuck the ends. The whole should then be served carefully and the finished knot will appear as in Fig. 120.

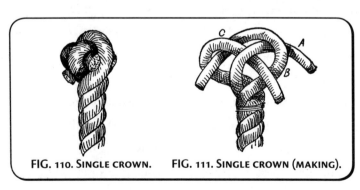

FIG. 110. SINGLE CROWN.   FIG. 111. SINGLE CROWN (MAKING).

FIG. 112. SINGLE CROWN
TUCKED (MAKING).

FIG. 113. SINGLE CROWN
TUCKED (COMPLETE).

FIG. 114. WALL KNOT.

FIG. 115. WALL KNOT
(MAKING).

FIG. 116. WALL KNOT (TUCKED).

FIG. 117. SHROUD KNOT (COMPLETE).

FIG. 118. SHROUD KNOT (MAKING).

FIG. 119. FRENCH SHROUD KNOT (MAKING).

FIG. 120. FRENCH SHROUD KNOT (COMPLETE).

Double wall and double crown as well as the beautiful double wall-and-crown knots are made exactly like the single crown or wall but instead of trimming off or tucking the ends they are carried around a second time following the lay of the first, as shown in Fig. 121, which shows the construction of a double crown at *A*, and a double wall at *B*. When finished, the ends may be tucked or trimmed and the two knots will look like Figs. 122 and 123. A far better effect is obtained by "Crowning" a wall knot. This is done by first making a single wall knot and then by bringing strand *A* up over the top and laying *B* across *A* and bringing *C* over *B* and through the bight of *A*; a crown knot is formed above the wall, as shown in Figs. 124 and 125. This is the foundation of the most beautiful of rope-end knots, known as the "Double Wall and Crown," or "Manrope Knot," illustrated in Fig. 126. Make your single wall and crown it, but leave the strands all slack; then pass the ends up and through the bights of the slack single-wall knot and then push them alongside the strands in the single crown; pushing them through the same bight in the crown and downward through the walling. This may seem quite difficult, but if you have learned the wall and crown you will find it simple enough, for it is really merely "following" the strands of the single wall and crown. The result, if properly done, and ends drawn tight and cut off closely, is surprising, and to the uninitiated most perplexing, for if the ends are tapered and tucked through the standing part of the ropes, as shown in Fig. 127, there will be no sign of a beginning or ending to this knot. This is probably the most useful of decorative knots and is largely used aboard ship for finishing the ends of rope railings, the ends of man-ropes, for the ends of yoke-lines and to form "stoppers" or "toggles" to bucket handles, slings, etc. Its use in this way is illustrated in Figs. 128–130, which show how to make a handy topsail-halyard toggle from an eye splice turned in a short piece of rope and finished with a double wall and crown at the end. These toggles are very useful about small boats, as they may be used as stops for furling sails, for slings around gaffs or spars, for hoisting, and in a variety of other ways which will at once suggest themselves to the boating man.

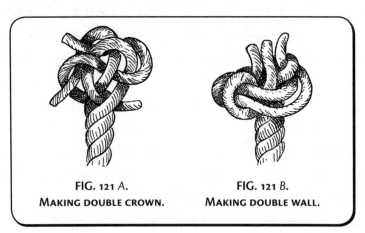

FIG. 121 A.
MAKING DOUBLE CROWN.

FIG. 121 B.
MAKING DOUBLE WALL.

FIG. 122. DOUBLE CROWN
(COMPLETE).

FIG. 123. DOUBLE WALL
(COMPLETE).

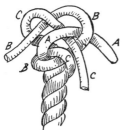

FIG. 124. WALL CROWNED
(MAKING).

FIG. 125. WALL CROWNED
(COMPLETE).

FIG. 126.
DOUBLE WALL AND CROWN.

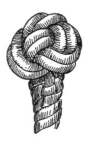

FIG. 127.
DOUBLE WALL AND CROWN
(COMPLETE).

The most difficult of ending knots and one which you should certainly learn is the "Matthew Walker" (Fig. 131), also known as the "Stopper Knot." To form this splendid knot, pass one strand around the standing part of the rope and through its own bight, then pass *B* underneath and through bight of *A* and through its own bight also; next pass *C* underneath and around and through the bights of *A*, *B*, and its own bight. The knot will now appear as in Fig. 132, but by carefully hauling the ends around and working the bight taut a little at a time the knot will assume the appearance shown in Fig. 133. This is a handsome and useful knot and is widely used on ends of ropes where they pass through holes, as for bucket handles, ropes for trap- door handles, chest handles, etc. The knot is well adapted for such purposes, as it is hard, close, and presents an almost flat shoulder on its lower side.

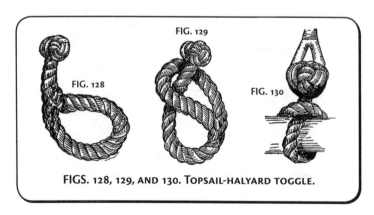

FIGS. 128, 129, AND 130. TOPSAIL-HALYARD TOGGLE.

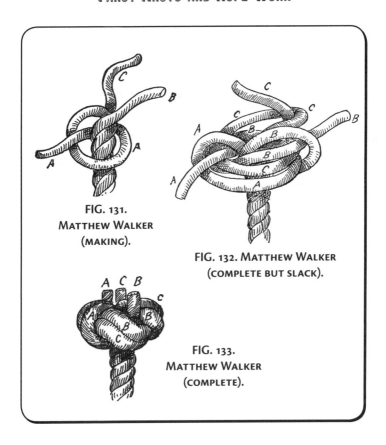

FIG. 131.
MATTHEW WALKER
(MAKING).

FIG. 132. MATTHEW WALKER
(COMPLETE BUT SLACK).

FIG. 133.
MATTHEW WALKER
(COMPLETE).

The "Turk's Head," Figs. 135 and 136, is a knot much used aboard yachts and warships and is so handsome and ornamental that it is a great favorite. It is used in ornamenting rigging, in forming shoulders or rings on stays or ropes to hold other gear in place, to ornament yoke lines, and for forming slip-collars on knife lanyards. It is also used to form collars around stanchions or spars, and, placed around a rope close beneath a man-rope knot, it gives a beautiful finish. When made of small line sailors often use the Turk's Head as a neckerchief fastener. Although so elaborate in effect, it is really an easy knot to make, and while you may have difficulty in getting it right at first a little patience and practice will enable you to become proficient and capable of tying it rapidly and easily in any place or position. To make a Turk's Head, have a smooth, round stick, or other object, and some closely twisted or braided small line. Pass two turns of the line around the rod, *A*, Fig. 135, from left to right, and pass the upper bight down through the lower and reeve the upper end down through it, as at *B*. Then pass the bight up again and run the end over the lower bight and up between it and the upper bight. Turn the upper bight again through the lower one and pass the end over what is now the upper bight and between it and the lower, *C*, Fig. 135. Now work from left to right, following the lay of the knot (or, in other words, passing your long end alongside the first end), *D*, Fig. 135, until a braid of two or more lays is completed, as shown in Fig. 136. The Turk's Head may be drawn as tight as desired around the rope, or rod, by working up the slack and drawing all bights taut. A variation of the knot may be formed by making the first part as described and then by slipping the knot to the end of the rod; work one side tighter than the other until the "Head" forms a complete cap, as shown in Fig. 137. This makes a splendid finish for the ends of flagpoles, stanchions, etc.

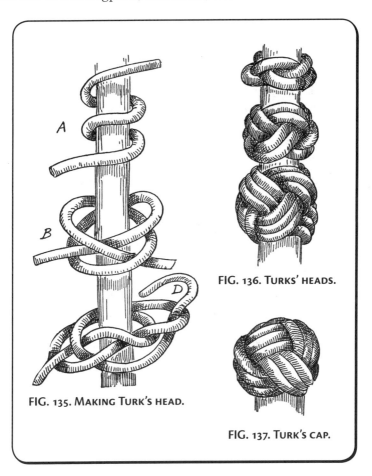

FIG. 136. TURKS' HEADS.

FIG. 135. MAKING TURK'S HEAD.

FIG. 137. TURK'S CAP.

Knots, Splices, and Rope Work

Ropes that are to be used as hand-lines, stanchions, man-ropes, railings, or in fact wherever a neat appearance counts, are usually wormed, served, and parcelled. Worming consists in twisting a small line into the grooves between the strands of rope, *A*, Fig. 138. This fills up the grooves and makes the rope smooth and ready for serving or parcelling. Parcelling consists in covering the rope already wormed with a strip of canvas wound spirally around it with the edges overlapping, *B*, Fig. 138. Serving is merely wrapping the rope with spun yarn, marline, or other small stuff, *C*, Fig. 138. Although this may all be done by hand, yet it can be accomplished far better by using a "Serving Mallet," shown in *D*, Fig. 138. This instrument enables you to work tighter and more evenly than by hand, but in either case you must have the rope to be served stretched tightly between two uprights. Often a rope is served without parcelling and for ordinary purposes parcelling is not required. A variation of serving is made by "half-hitch" work, as shown in Figs. 139–140. This is very pretty when well done and is very easy to accomplish. Take a half-hitch around the rope to be served, then another below it; draw snug; take another half-hitch and so on until the object is covered and the series of half-hitch knots forms a spiral twist, as shown in the illustrations. Bottles, jugs, ropes, stanchions, fenders, and numerous other articles may be covered with half-hitch work; and as you become more expert you will be able to use several lines of half-hitches at the same time.

Four-strand braiding is also highly ornamental and is easy and simple. The process is illustrated in Fig. 141, and consists in crossing the opposite strands across and past one another, as shown in *A, B, C,* Fig 141. Still more ornamental is the "Crown-braid" which appears, when finished, as in Fig. 143. The process of forming this braid is exactly like ordinary crowning and does not require any description; it may be done with any number of strands, but four or six are usually as many as the beginner cares to handle at one time.

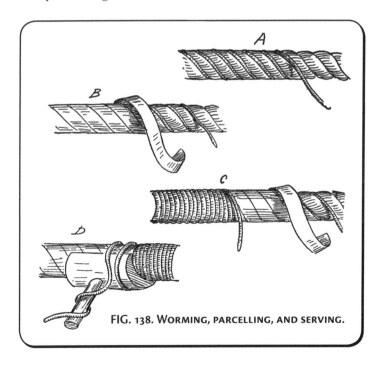

FIG. 138. WORMING, PARCELLING, AND SERVING.

FIG. 139.
HALF-HITCH WORK.

FIG. 140.
HALF-HITCH WORK.

FIG. 141. FOUR-STRAND BRAID (MAKING).

FIG. 142. FOUR-STRAND BRAID (COMPLETE).

FIG. 143. CROWN-BRAID.

When the rope-worker has mastered all the knots, ties, bends, hitches, and splices I have described, he will find a new field open to the use of rope in innumerable ways. Barrels, casks, bales, or other objects may be roped, or slung, with ease and security; ropes will be pressed into service for straps and belts; and buckles may be readily formed by the simple expedient shown in Fig. 144. If a swivel is required it can be arranged as shown in Fig. 145, while several simple slings are illustrated in Figs. 146–148. In a factory, or machine shop, rope belting will often prove far better than leather, and if well spliced together will run very smoothly and evenly even on long stretches. As a recreation for killing time aboard ship, or on rainy vacation days, few occupations will prove more enjoyable than tying fancy knots and making new splices and bends or inventing new variations of the numerous hitches, ties, and knots you already know.

FIG. 144. ROPE BUCKLE.

FIG. 145. SWIVELS.

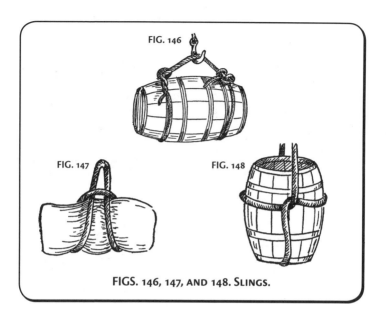

FIG. 146

FIG. 147

FIG. 148

FIGS. 146, 147, AND 148. SLINGS.

HALTERS FOR ANIMALS

Every now and then a temporary halter is needed for a horse, and in Fig. 149 such a halter is shown. This halter is made by putting the end of a long rope around the neck of the horse and then tying a common bow-line knot. (See Fig. 150.) Fig. 151 shows the second step to be followed, that of passing the rope around the animal's head twice, while Fig. 152 shows how the second loop is passed under the first. In Fig. 153 the rope is shown sufficiently long enough to enable it to be passed over the ears of the animal and leave the halter completed, as shown in Fig. 154.

FIG. 149.

PUT A LOOP OVER THE
HORSE'S NOSE.

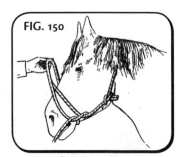

FIG. 150

THE "BOWLINE" KNOT.

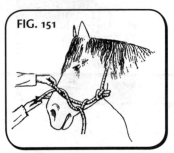

FIG. 151

FOLLOW THIS WITH A
SECOND LOOP.

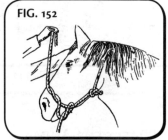

FIG. 152

PASS THE SECOND LOOP
UNDER THE FIRST.

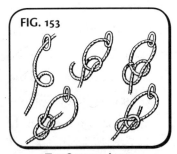

FIG. 153

THE SECOND LOOP
SHOULD BE LONG.

FIG. 154

IT GOES OVER THE
FORELOCK AND EARS.